## Dedicated to:
## Jen, Ryan, & Lucy

Written By: Abigail Gartland

# I was born in Israel around the time that Jesus was born.

# Hello, my name is St. Jude!

# I was one of the 12 apostles of Jesus.

This is my brother, James. We both followed Jesus during His life.

I am known to have a flame over my head in pictures.

The flame represents Pentecost, when I accepted the Holy Spirit to lead me in my life.

On my travels with Jesus, I saw Him perform many miracles.

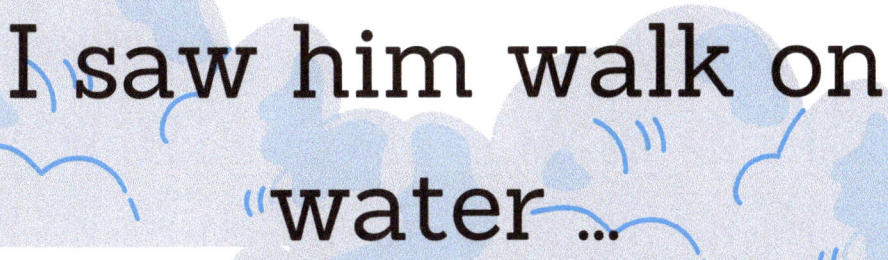

# I saw him walk on water ...

I saw Him multiply the loaves and the fishes ..

I even saw him resurrected on the third day after he died.

I spent my whole life loving Jesus and watching Him work to save us. I am blessed that Jesus chose me to follow Him.

# Do you want to be more like me?

You can celebrate my feast day with me on October 28th

# I am the patron saint of impossible causes.

# I pray for you every day of your life.

# St. Jude, Pray for Us

## Copyright:

Clipart: © PentoolPixie  © LimeandKiwiDesigns
Licensed purchased: 1/10/2024

# About the Author

## Abigail Gartland

I love the saints and I love my faith. The idea for sharing the stories of the saints with little ones came when my dear friends were expecting their first baby. I wanted to create something as unique and special as our friendship. Each book is dedicated to very special people and groups who have enriched my faith in different ways. I am blessed to write these stories and appreciate the unending support of my family and friends. When I am not writing, I am a middle school teacher. I hope you enjoy these stories. I pray for each and every person who opens one of my books to learn more about the saints.

*Abbie*

www.ingramcontent.com/pod-product-compliance
Lightning Source LLC
LaVergne TN
LVHW061633070526
838199LV00071B/6666